I0815444

The Right to Play

How Jane Addams Fought for America's Playgrounds

Elizabeth Brown

illustrated by Olga Lee

Albert Whitman & Company
Chicago, Illinois

For Chesney, Michael, Sylvia, and Alessandra—EB

To my mother and father, Eleonora and Nickolay Lee—OL

Library of Congress Cataloging-in-Publication data is on file with the publisher.

Illustrations by Olga Lee
First published in the United States of America in 2025 by Albert Whitman & Company
ISBN 978-0-8075-7074-6 (hardcover)
ISBN 978-0-8075-7075-3 (ebook)

Printed in the United States of America
10 9 8 7 6 5 4 3 2 1 TR 30 29 28 27 26 25

Design by Erin McMahon

For more information about Albert Whitman & Company, visit our website at www.albertwhitman.com

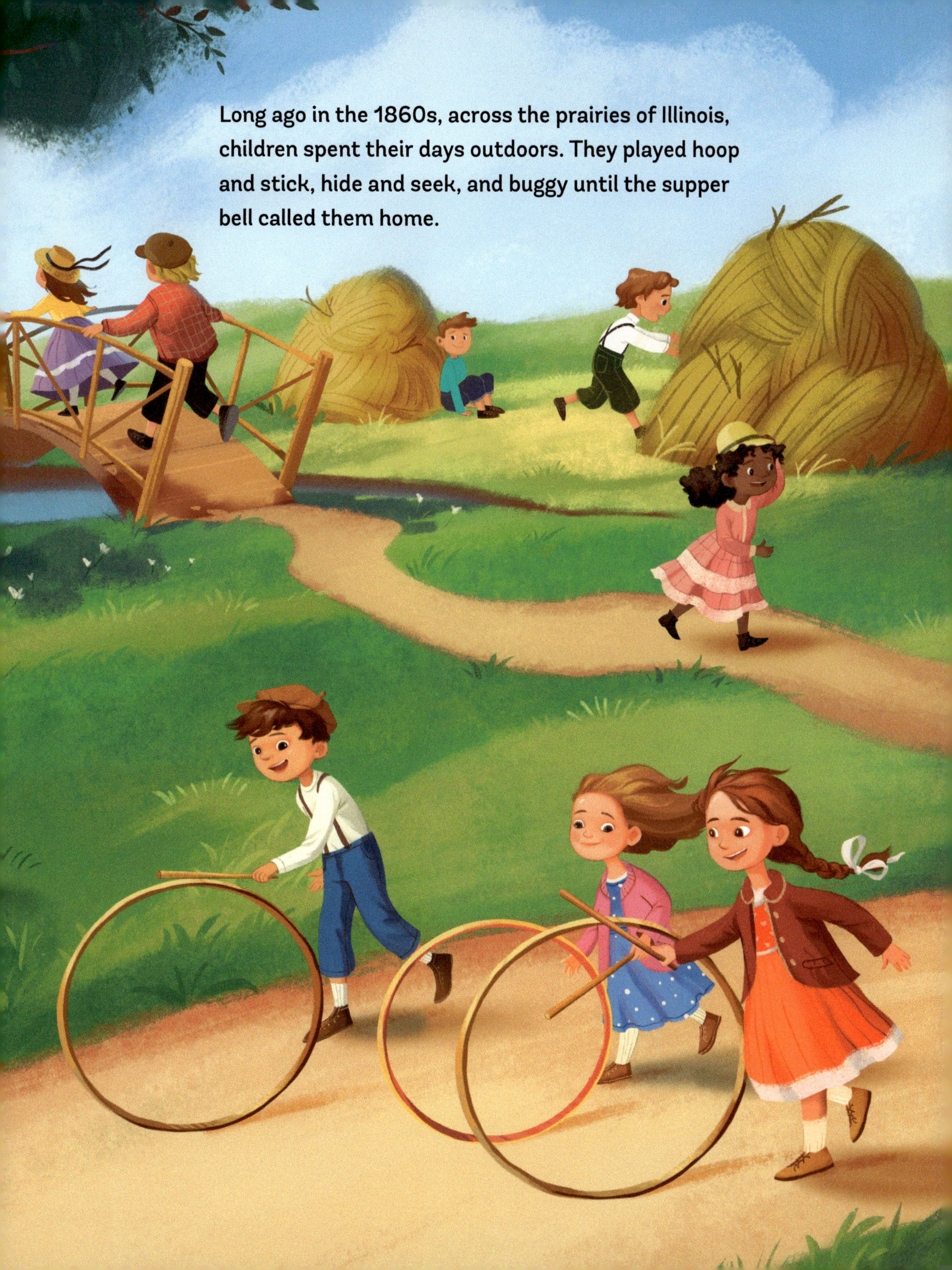

Long ago in the 1860s, across the prairies of Illinois, children spent their days outdoors. They played hoop and stick, hide and seek, and buggy until the supper bell called them home.

But not Jane Addams. At five years old, she had a limp and couldn't run well. Her toes turned in, and her spine was crooked from the tuberculosis she'd had when she was four. Watching her friends and brother from the window, Jane felt different and alone.

"I want to play, too!" Jane said.
"I want to run and jump with my friends."

By the time she was six, Jane was well enough to play. Skipping as fast as she could, Jane couldn't wait to join a game of tag. Would she be welcome, even if she couldn't run as fast as the other children?

The answer was yes.

Next...hopscotch.

"I did it!" Jane said.

Then, jump rope, scavenger hunt, fort!

"Let's play again tomorrow! I can't wait!" Jane shouted as she waved to her friends at the end of the day.

Play made Jane stronger, and she made new friends. By summer's end, she dashed across the prairie with all the other children.

But Jane never forgot what it felt like to be left out. While driving through nearby towns with her father, she saw families living in run-down shacks and barefoot, hungry children with no space to run.

A different life than her own. Jane had felt left out from other children, but these children had been left out of a childhood. She promised herself that when she grew up, she'd be a good neighbor to everyone, inviting others to her house to read, learn...and play.

Jane grew up and kept her word. After college, she spent time in London, England, where she visited Toynbee Hall. Toynbee was no ordinary home. It was a settlement house that helped immigrants—people from other countries—make new lives for themselves. It offered English classes, healthcare, and job training. After returning to America, Jane and her friend Ellen Gates Starr founded their own settlement house just west of downtown Chicago. They called it Hull House.

Outside Hull House, the city screeched and blared. Tenement buildings loomed like giants around it. Factory assembly lines *whirred* as Jane's immigrant neighbors from countries such as Italy, Germany, Poland, Russia, Mexico, and Ireland labored long hours for little pay, building new lives while helping to build America.

Inside Hull House, hope blossomed, and help was always ready. Jane provided healthcare, washtubs, and English lessons for the immigrant families. She understood the struggles they faced from her time at Toynbee Hall, and she always listened, encouraging people to listen to each other, too, despite their different traditions, languages, and customs.

Jane felt that a strong nation starts by caring for its children...*all* its children.

How could she make them feel welcome? How could she let children be kids?

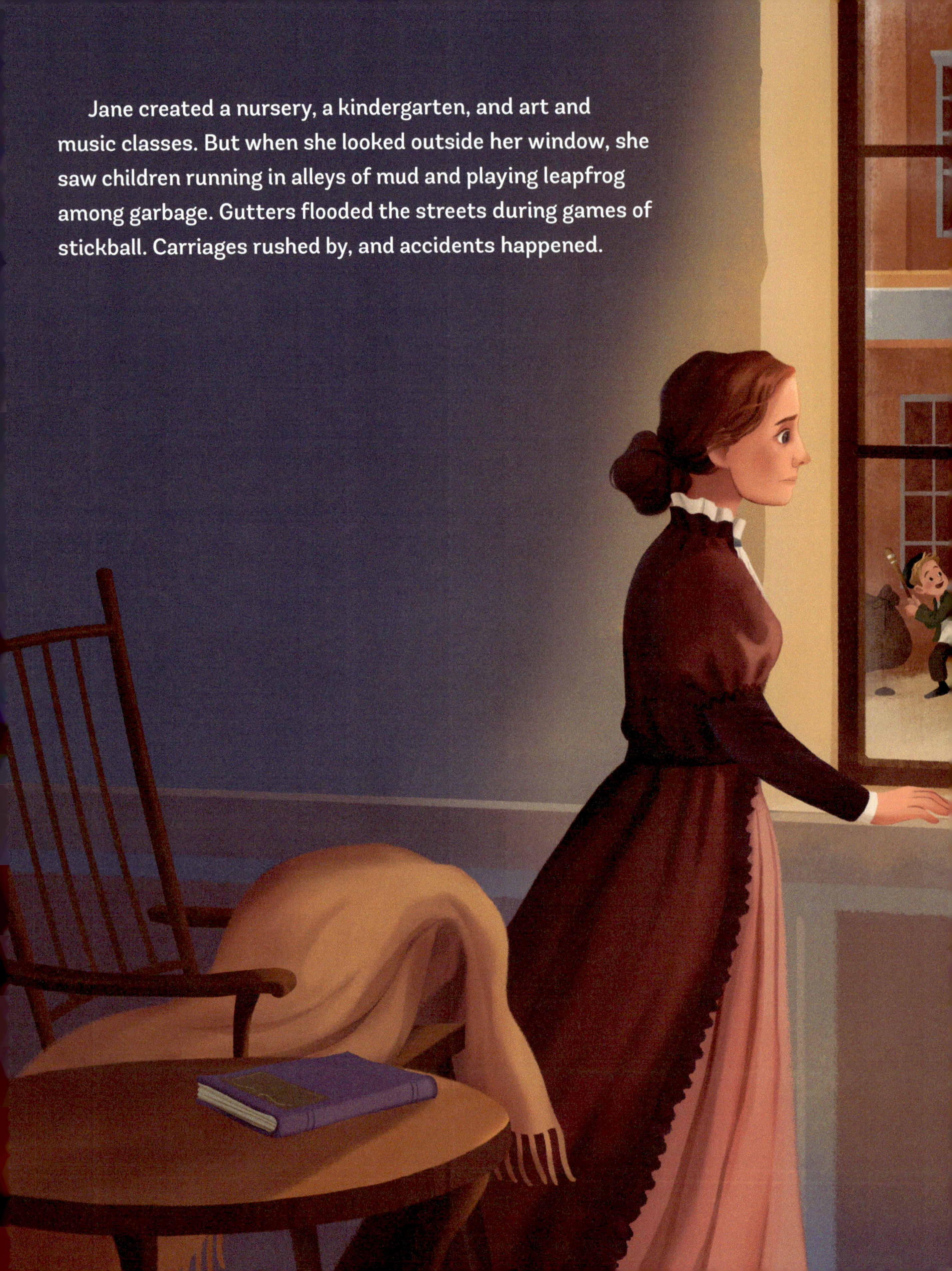

Jane created a nursery, a kindergarten, and art and music classes. But when she looked outside her window, she saw children running in alleys of mud and playing leapfrog among garbage. Gutters flooded the streets during games of stickball. Carriages rushed by, and accidents happened.

Jane longed to see children playing like she had as a girl, safe and free. Remembering the outdoor gymnasiums she'd seen during her time in Europe, Jane came up with a plan and bargained with a wealthy man to give her the lot he owned near Hull House.

Workers tore the crumbling buildings down and leveled the land. They sawed. They hammered. The *clang* of steel against steel rang like a trumpet heralding good news. Children watched and wondered. At last, it was real...

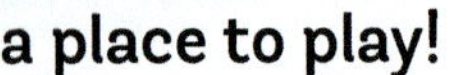

a place to play!

This was one of the first model playgrounds in America—one with equipment for play—the design from which all others would be built.

People around the country heard about this playground.

Newspapers praised Jane. Her playground brought progress.

You go first! I'll go next because you haven't swung yet.

Remember to share.

Everyone will get a turn.

Children (and their imaginations) ran free, making up games, stories, and worlds to explore. They learned how to work out problems and differences at the playground.

Jane created sports teams and activities to bring more children together, such as planting trees, celebrating birthday parties and holidays with marching bands, and holding play festivals to learn games from each other's countries.

For children with disabilities, a matter close to her heart, Jane helped design playground equipment, sand gardens, and programs to help all experience the joy of play.

Sun warming faces. Sand squishing through toes. Playgrounds delighted the senses and spirit. They strengthened the body.

But cities grew.

Space was scarce.

Many Americans didn't like that Jane was setting aside so much valuable land for immigrant children to play. They created neighborhood watches to report her and petitions to stop her.

Go back to your countries!

Neighbor argued with neighbor.

Immigrants shouldn't have rights!

Elected to one of the highest offices in the newly formed Playground Association of America in 1906, Jane fought back. Children couldn't wait. Playgrounds brought kids together when society pulled them apart. *All* children deserve to play!

Jane launched a movement to build playgrounds across the country. City planners scouted for land. Architects joined her, designing the spaces for fun and testing them for safety.

Still, America had work to do. Immigrant and poor children across the country worked in fields and factories from dawn to dark. Jane formed the National Child Labor Committee in 1907, investigating factories, taking photos, and showing everyone what children had lost.

Factories protested.

Stay out of our affairs!

They rallied against her ideas.

Mind your own business!

Next, Jane spoke out to community leaders and politicians, calling on governments to ban businesses from selling products made from child labor and closing down factories that hired children. Jane's efforts helped pass the Federal Child Labor Law in 1916. Now, children had what should have *always* been theirs: the chance to play, the time to play!

Jane didn't stop there. She used her pen to fight, writing books and donating the money to help her cause. Playgrounds were as important as schools in helping children grow up happy and healthy. Jane believed that childhood mattered.

"Give all children the opportunity to be children," Jane said. "Let children play!"

This time, people listened.

New laws passed. Cities built playgrounds that children could walk to without danger—in every community across the country. More swings! More slides! More play!

Sprawling across America, playgrounds grew larger and safer—in schoolyards, in parks, and with community houses offering recreation for the whole family.

No matter how they changed, one thing remained the same: playgrounds built friendships.

Throughout the rest of her life, Jane Addams fought for women's rights, civil rights, and world peace.

But she never stopped fighting for playgrounds. Her work ensured *all* children the right to play!

Jane fought for *you*!

AUTHOR'S NOTE

All her life, Jane Addams helped others. She fought to win voting rights for women, promoted world peace, and worked tirelessly for social reforms that bettered countless lives. All the while, she believed that play and recreation were as important to children as school and that all children should have access to playgrounds. Jane gave immigrant children places to play. She opened summer camps with playgrounds for children to swing, climb, and slide in the crisp country air. She even opened the first public swimming pool.

Jane used her knowledge of design and model playgrounds to help communities understand the benefits of playground equipment and how to go about designing and constructing the playgrounds.

But Jane didn't stop there. In keeping with her beliefs that children should be allowed to be children, she worked tirelessly to end child labor, allowing children to hope, dream, and play.

Jane never stopped working hard for children and playgrounds. She won the Nobel Peace Prize in 1931.